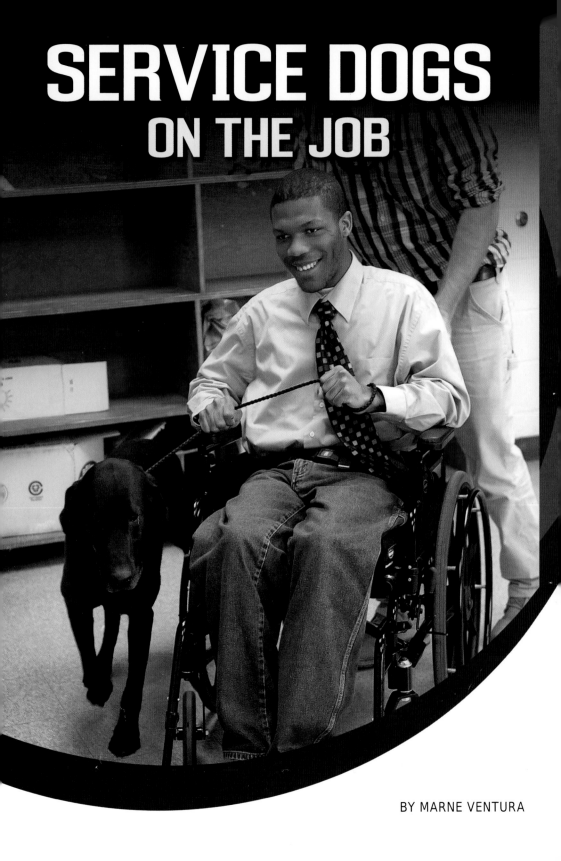

SERVICE DOGS
ON THE JOB

BY MARNE VENTURA

The Child's World®
childsworld.com

Published by The Child's World®
1980 Lookout Drive • Mankato, MN 56003-1705
800-599-READ • www.childsworld.com

Photographs ©: John Byrum/Spartanburg Herald-Journal/AP Images,
cover, 1; John Taylor/Rex/Newscom, 5; Tonya Doughty/iStockphoto, 6;
Shutterstock Images, 9; Huntstock/Thinkstock, 10, 12; iStockphoto, 13, 17;
Cpl. Lisa Tourtelot/Marine Air Station Miramar/3rd Marine Aircraft Wing,
14; Heather L. Smith/Aurora Sentinel/AP Images, 16; Serguei Kovalev/
iStockphoto, 18; LiAndStudio/Shutterstock Images, 20

ISBN 9781503816169

LCCN 2016945602

Printed in the United States of America
PA02318

TABLE OF
CONTENTS

Fast Facts 4

Chapter 1
Stuck in the Mud 7

Chapter 2
Making a Hero..........................11

Chapter 3
Hero Saves the Day 19

Think About It 21
Glossary 22
To Learn More 23
Selected Bibliography 23
Index 24
About the Author 24

FAST FACTS

The Job

- Guide dogs help blind people move about safely.
- Hearing dogs alert deaf people to sounds.
- **Mobility** dogs help people in wheelchairs.
- **Seizure** alert dogs help people with **epilepsy**.
- **Autism** dogs comfort and calm children with autism.

Training Time

- A service dog learns to do tasks a person with a **disability** cannot.
- Training takes six months to one year.
- The dogs must obey basic commands.
- They must respond when called.
- Service dogs are trained to have good social skills.

Common Breeds

- Labrador retrievers
- Golden retrievers
- German shepherds

Famous Dogs

- Buddy was the first official guide dog for a blind person. Her owner, Morris Frank, helped start the first school to train guide dogs.

- Roselle was a guide dog in New York City on September 11, 2001. She led her owner, Michael Hingson, to safety when the World Trade Center was attacked.

- Endal was a service dog who had failed his training at first. Alan Parton was in a wheelchair from war injuries. He could not remember his wife and children. Endal befriended Alan and helped him regain his life.

Chapter 1

STUCK IN THE MUD

Hero jogged next to 36-year-old Gareth Jones's wheelchair. The four-year-old golden retriever sniffed the air and wagged his tail. He looked around the English countryside and then back at his owner. Hero was always ready for fresh air and exercise. It was his job. Jones's arms and legs had been hurt in a car accident. Hero helped Jones get around in his wheelchair.

Some days, Jones had too much pain to go for a stroll. He had to rest. On those days, Hero lay with Jones. He put his chin on Jones's chest. Jones knew Hero missed going outside, but Hero never complained.

Today, Jones felt well enough to go outside. He chose to go on a trail where no vehicles could go.

◄ Golden retrievers are calm and strong, important qualities for service dogs.

Along the trail, Jones saw an open gate. It led to a field he'd never noticed. It would be fun to explore, he thought. He rolled his wheelchair through. Hero trotted after him. A toy with a ball attached to a rope dangled from Hero's mouth.

Soon, Jones saw a shadow on the ground. He looked up. Rain clouds were moving in. He knew it was time to return home. Jones tried to move his wheelchair. He felt the wheels stick in the mud. The wheelchair would not budge. Worse yet, he had left his cell phone at home.

Jones called for Hero, and the dog ran to his side. The rope-toy hung from Hero's mouth. Jones's heart thumped against his chest. His wife did not know where he was. Nobody else would be traveling nearby in the rain. How long would he be stuck in the storm before someone found him?

Service dogs help people in wheelchairs go where they ▶ otherwise might not.

Chapter 2

MAKING A HERO

Hero started training as a service dog when he was a puppy. When he was about 14 months old, he started training with a special teacher. He learned to obey basic commands, such as *sit* and *stay*. Then he started to learn how to be a mobility dog. He learned to bring things to a person in a wheelchair. He learned commands such as *pull*. He learned how to turn a light switch on or off.

By the time Hero met Jones, he had learned to do 100 tasks that Jones could not do for himself. Usually a dog is assigned to a person in need. In Hero's case, he picked Jones. He ran up to him, wagging his tail. He was **eager** to work with Jones. He even stayed by his side during training breaks.

◄ Mobility dogs must learn to do many tasks before they are assigned to a person.

▲ **Homes can be adapted so that dogs can do more things for their owners.**

Tine was a golden retriever bred to be a guide dog. Like Hero, Tine first learned to be **obedient**. Then when Tine was 16 months old, he learned to wear a harness and lead a blind person. This took two to three months of practice. When Tine passed all the tests, he was given to a blind woman named Sally Dodge.

Dodge's eyes filled with tears the first time she met Tine. She was so happy to have a dog to help her. When she reached out to touch him he licked her hand. Dodge said Tine was her eyes and her best friend.

▲ **Guide dogs help their owners navigate around objects.**

Dominic, a German shepherd hearing dog, learned at home to be a service dog. He sat by his owner, Linda Lohdefinck, while she worked at her desk. When there was a knock on the door or the phone rang, he put his paw on her knee to get her attention. Then he led her to the source of the sound.

Some dogs are born with certain skills that help them become service dogs. For example, some dogs know when someone is about to have a seizure. These dogs paw and bark at, circle around, or lick people before they seize. Trainers reward the dogs for this behavior. The dogs learn to stay close to their owners and warn them before they have seizures. The person with epilepsy can lie down or ask for help before the seizure, to avoid getting hurt. The dog can even go get another family member for help. Eight-year-old Spencer's seizure dog Lucia stays with him all night. Lucia goes to wake up Spencer's mom or dad before he has a seizure. That way, they can come and make sure Spencer is safe.

Seizure dogs are always ready to help people with epilepsy. ▶

For autism dogs, the trainer first teaches one or both of the autistic child's parents to work with the dog. They learn how to give the dog commands and understand the dog's behavior.

▲ **Autism dogs can help kids stay calm.**

▲ **Service dogs are trained to stay at their owners' sides.**

The dog and parent spend time getting to know each other. Next the dog goes home with the parent. For a week or two, the dog and the child get to know each other. Then a trainer visits. The trainer works with the dog and child every day for a week. The trainer teaches the dog what to do if a child wanders away, or gets upset in a crowd, or cannot go to sleep.

Chapter 3

HERO SAVES THE DAY

The sky darkened over Jones and Hero. Jones tried again to move his wheelchair out of the mud. It would not budge.

Hero whined. He put his head on Jones's lap. The ball-on-a-rope was still in his mouth. The damp rope fell across Jones's leg.

Jones stared at the top of his faithful dog's head and thought about what to do next. Then it came to him. He told Hero to drop the ball onto his lap. Then Jones wrapped the end of the rope around the side of the wheelchair. After a lot of work, he was able to make a loop and tie it.

◀ Service dogs are trained to pay close attention to their owners.

▲ Mobility dogs are trained to be forceful
when necessary.

Jones told Hero to pull. Hero wagged his tail. He
took the ball in his mouth and gently tugged. As a
well-trained service dog, Hero was always careful with
Jones. But this time, Jones needed Hero to pull hard.

Jones told Hero to pull again. Hero understood.
It was okay to be forceful this time. With the ball in
his mouth, Hero backed away from Jones. The rope
tightened. But the wheelchair still did not move.

Hero did not let up. He braced his back legs
and pulled harder. His paws dug into the ground.

Jones spoke to his dog, telling him to keep trying. Jones felt the wheelchair start to move. Hero pulled harder. Soon Hero had pulled the wheelchair onto dry ground. By the time they got home, both Hero and Jones were covered with mud. But Jones was safe and dry.

The British government gave Hero an All-Star Animal Award for rescuing Jones. Hero showed off his training at the ceremony. When they gave him the award, he sat up straight and held out his paw to shake.

THINK ABOUT IT

- German shepherds, golden retrievers, and Labrador retrievers are all big dogs. Why is being big important for a mobility dog?
- Guide dogs and hearing dogs are trained to focus on the person they are helping. How can others help these dogs do their jobs?
- Do you think it's a good idea to offer a treat to a service dog? Why or why not?

GLOSSARY

autism (AW-tiz-um): Autism is a disorder that makes it hard to talk to and be with other people. Some service dogs help children with autism stay calm around others.

disability (dis-uh-BIL-i-tee): A disability is a condition that limits or stops someone's ability to do something. Mobility dogs help disabled people in wheelchairs move about.

eager (EE-gur): To be eager is to show happiness or enthusiasm. The guide dog was eager to meet the blind girl he would be helping.

epilepsy (EP-uh-lep-see): Epilepsy is a disorder that causes seizures. Seizure dogs alert people with epilepsy of oncoming seizures.

mobility (moh-BIL-i-tee): Mobility is the state of being able to move around. Mobility dogs help people in wheelchairs by opening and closing doors.

obedient (oh-BEE-dee-unt): To be obedient is to follow directions. It is important for a service dog to be obedient.

seizure (SEE-zur): A seizure is a sudden attack caused by abnormal brain activity. A seizure dog can alert a person before the person has a seizure.

TO LEARN MORE

Books

Green, Sara. *Service Dogs*. Minneapolis, MN: Bellwether, 2014.

Hoffman, Mary Ann. *Helping Dogs*. New York: Gareth Stevens, 2011.

Montalván, Luis Carlos, and Bret Witter. *Tuesday Tucks Me In*. New York: Roaring Brook, 2014.

Web Sites

Visit our Web site for links about service dogs: childsworld.com/links

Note to Parents, Teachers, and Librarians: We routinely verify our Web links to make sure they are safe and active sites. So encourage your readers to check them out!

SELECTED BIBLIOGRAPHY

"Endal: The Amazing Assistance Dog." *National Geographic*. National Geographic Channel, 2016. Web. 8 Jun. 2016.

Jones, Gareth P. "Animal Hero: Hero, a Dog." *MyHero.com*. Hero Project, 26 Aug. 2010. Web. 8 Jun. 2016.

"Personal Story of a Seizure Dog." *Epilepsy.com*. Epilepsy Foundation, 2008. Web. 8 Jun. 2016.

"What Are the Minimum Training Standards for a Service Dog?" *AnythingPawsable.com*. Anything Pawsable, 2015. Web. 8 Jun. 2016.

INDEX

All-Star Animal Award, 21

autism dog, 4, 16

Buddy (dog), 5

disability, 4

Dodge, Sally, 12–13

Dominic (dog), 14

Endal (dog), 5

epilepsy, 4, 14

German shepherd, 4, 14, 21

golden retriever, 4, 7, 12, 21

guide dog, 4–5, 12, 21

hearing dog, 4, 14, 21

Hero (dog), 7–8, 11–12, 19–21

Hingson, Michael, 5

Jones, Gareth, 7–8, 11, 19–21

Labrador retriever, 4, 21

Lohdefinck, Linda, 14

Lucia (dog), 14

mobility dog, 4, 11, 21

Morris, Frank, 5

Parton, Alan, 5

Roselle (dog), 5

seizure alert dog, 4, 14

Tine (dog), 12–13

trainer, 14, 16–17

ABOUT THE AUTHOR

Marne Ventura is the author of 37 books for kids. She loves writing about nature, science, technology, health, food, and crafts. She is a former elementary school teacher, and she holds a master's degree in education. Marne lives with her husband on the central coast of California.